ZOMBIES!

EVACUATE THE SCHOOL!

ZOMBIES!

EVACUATE THE SCHOOL!

SARA HOLBROOK

ILLUSTRATIONS BY

KAREN SANDSTROM

WORDSONG

HONESDALE, PENNSYLVANIA

CONTENTS

A FEW WORDS ABOUT ZOMBIES, POETRY, AND OTHER STUFF

What? You think zombies were in my school when I was a kid? I wish. An occasional zombie would have been a pretty great diversion from my two most memorable school-zone pastimes—perfecting my fake sneeze and pushing the drool around in my mouth with my tongue, trying to look interested while my mind was outside on the playground.

In school I was never what some people think you should be, which is perfect. Everyone knows you get points off for anything less than perfection. I bet you think that I went to a perfect school with perfect teachers and that I was even perfecter than all of them added up together. That I got all A's and was like a jack-in-the-box on awards day, popping up to shake the principal's hand and collecting stacks of certificates to post on my bedroom wall next to all the blue ribbons I got from playing the violin.

A. I can't play the violin.
B. I never got all A's. Not even once.

If you count being quiet as being good at school, then I was pretty good (*Aaaaa-choo!*). I did most of my worksheets. I was afraid not to. I wasn't in the top reading group, but I still remember that Christopher Columbus bobbed across the ocean to the New World in 1492, how to conjugate verbs, and that Otto Mergenthaler invented the linotype machine, so I can't honestly say that school was a waste. Even though my school days were littered with mind-sucking black holes, I did learn stuff.

What I did **not** learn in school was how to write poetry. The first poem I remember writing that was not for an assignment was about how it felt to be blind. Guess I tuned out the *write what you know* part of that lesson. There were no real reasons in my life to play the sympathy card, so I just made one up for poetry purposes because it seemed like the right thing to do. Poetry is supposed to be happy or sad—or so I thought at the time—and my life was seriously medium. Could be I was looking for poetry to put a little drama in my boring life, or maybe I was just a little nuts.

Kids start out a little nuts and then become more nuts as they turn into grown-ups. Take my teacher at Anderson Middle School, Mrs. Housch. She was about 112, wore lace-up high heels and her eyeglasses on a string around her neck. She galloped around the room when she read us Henry Wadsworth Longfellow's poem *The Midnight Ride of Paul Revere*, her glasses bouncing up and down. She was what's called in poetry an *image*—a mind-picture that sticks with you. I didn't realize what a good image she was until years later when I still remembered what she looked like. Mrs. Housch turned out to be an image that stuck with me for a long time, like a mosquito-bite scar.

After her gallop around the room, Mrs. Housch announced that there would be no worksheets for homework that week. We each were to write a poem and it was due on Friday. That was my poetry-writing lesson.

I was clueless. Write a poem? I'd gotten pretty good at filling in the blanks, but how was I supposed to write a poem? When I looked around the class and saw all the perfecter kids get busy writing, I froze up as solid as a pant leg in a bike chain. I wasn't going anywhere.

So that night at home, I went to the bookshelf and pulled a dusty, ancient poetry book with all kinds of loose threads hanging off it and copied a poem out of it about autumn and turned it in. I made sure I had some major erasures here and there to show how hard I'd worked on it. I think I tore the page in one place. It was perfection.

My luck. Mrs. Housch, with a few loose threads of her own, was older than that book. She knew the poem, the book it was swiped out of, and that I'd signed my pencil-smeared name to it. Busted. Points off. Story of my life.

My punishment was to write another poem, only this time using my own words. Can you believe that being a poet is now my job since the first poetry-writing experience I remember was dealt out as a punishment? True story.

The thing is, you never know what's going to stick out of your whole school experience or what lessons are going to help you later in life. Turns out, my tendency toward daydreaming has been a real plus, and it didn't really matter if Housch taught me how to write poetry. Writing poetry is something I had to learn on my own.

Knowing that, I decided to put this book together with the idea that, as writers, we are all teaching ourselves along the way. We do that through our reading and experimenting with words. So, included in this book, along with images of school, are some ideas on how you might try using some of my poems as models for your own writing, kind of like the way people sing other people's songs before they write their own.

And here's another fact I've picked up: as a writer, the awful boredom I dreaded as a kid is now my friend. In order to be a writer, I have to carve time out of my day—time away from the TV and my past-due deadlines—to be bored and see what my brain comes up with. Mind-skate time, I call it. Mind-skate time is leisure time, a concept that in the age of flat screens, video games, and earbuds has almost become extinct. That element of writing (leisure time) is as important as pencil and paper.

So take this book, find yourself some paper, pencil, and leisure time, and let yourself get bored. I'm waiting to hear from you.

BACK TO SCHOOL!

I've rewatched every rerun.
I have no skin on my knees.
I've had it with the crickets,
the sunburn, and the bees.

I hiked around the woods
and got peed on by a tree toad.
My neighbor took me fishing.
I got gang-jumped by mosquitoes.

I've been bitten, scorched, and stung,
and the ball field is a sneeze.
My controller went on strike, and
I'm bouncing off the trees.
Days, no longer long,
whisper, *Time to move along.*
School is calling, no use stalling.
Fall is falling, and it
cannot be ignored.
Should I follow?
Might as well.
I'm pretty bored.

COUNT DOWN TO GET UP

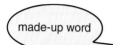
made-up word

Beneath
a hug of covers,
snugglebuggled
in my bed,
I count down—
ready . . . set—
I'm gonna get up. . . .
Instead,
I beg for two more minutes
from my heartless,
ticking clock.
I'm about as energetic
as a ten-ton moss-grown rock.

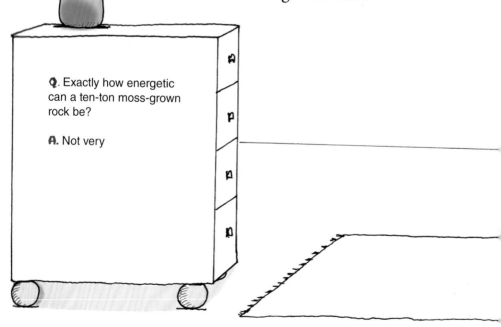

Q. Exactly how energetic can a ten-ton moss-grown rock be?

A. Not very

As I pass
my last
drop deadline,
I snugglebuggle deeper.
Why must I be up for learning?
I'm a summa-cum-laude sleeper.

A word about made-up words

In poetry, we can break the rules, sometimes using things like incomplete sentences and (rarely) made-up words. It's okay. Here's the trick: make sure you create a word people can understand. I never create nonsense words just to make a rhyme pattern work. A fake rhyme is like a fake smile—no one believes it. If you wonder if others will understand what you've written, show it to someone and ask, "Do you get this?" And if they don't, make changes. My favorite made-up wordsmith is Dr. Seuss, of course.

OVER THE LIMIT

LATE!
A panic fills my chest,
and no space left to breathe.
HURRY!
Tap-tap-**LATE!**
and
why'd I wait so **LATE!** to leave?

I'M LATE!
Just great.
I thought I had a bulging pocket-full-of-time
and plenty left to spend,
until I checked the time
and saw
the clock was not my friend.

LATE!
I've got to learn my limit.
LATE!
It hurts to have no breath.
LATE!
I've got to break the habit
LATE!
of causing me such stress.

Gee.
What word did I
use over and over
in this poem?

THE BUS STOP

Race.
Chase.
Hurry.
Scurry.
Stand.
Wait.
Don't be late.
The bus stops here,
beside this sign.
Now watch,
and hope,
it comes
on time.

A refrain is a repeated word or phrase. Musicians use refrains in songs, too, but they usually aren't just a single word or note.

BiG YELLOW PAiN

THUMP, BUMP, BUMP,
BOOM
This
BUMP, THUMP, THUMP
hurts.
SLAM
A backslap to start,
BAM
it stops me face first.
BUMP
The front's not that great,
WHAM
but the back is the worst!
JERKS
JUMP
Me bumping 'round corners.
SLIDES
SLIP
OOPS
Me side-to-side.
POP
PLOP
I'm just the pop balls

WHOA
on this pull-toy ride.
BOOM
BASH
It drops without warning,
WHAM!
springs me from the seat.
Airborne!
Airborne!
Suspending midair,
CRASH
BAM
slam-dancing my feet.
BOOM
BASH
It scrambles my breakfast.
OOPS
YISH
It chatters my brain
OUCH!
SMASH
and bruises my teeth.
Scoo, scoo, school bus!
BAM!
What a big yellow pain.

A third-grader once told me that she had to sit in the back of the bus, and she said, holding her stomach, "The back is the worst." Every poem is a blend of what we see and what we remember, so I mixed her words with my own memories of school-bus rides (yish) to write this bumpin', thumpin', onomatopoeia-jumpin' poem. That means I chose words—*pop, plop*—because they sound like what they really are.

What different sounds would you hear if you weren't bumping on a school bus but sliding across the water in a kayak or zooming down the sidewalk on skates?

MY SCHOOL

This is my school.
My front door.
My hall.
My gym.
My playground.
My basketball.
My markers.
My flag.
My hook, my book.
My desk, my mess,
and that's my book bag.
That window and I
have each other's back.
It breathes fresh and familiar
when opened a crack.
     The creak of the swings.
     The rustle of trees.
     The rumble of buses.
     Occasional bees. YIKES!
My school is where I spend my day,
read and add and take away.
My clock I watch
till recess time.
More than any other place in town,
     this place,
this school
is mine.

This is what is called a list poem. It's kind of a grocery list of observations. The American poet Walt Whitman is credited with creating this form, but I think lists have been around since someone needed to collect tools to build a pyramid.

Can you think of something in your life that you could make a list about and turn it into a poem? It could be a place (like a school), or it could be the gear you need to play a sport or what you don't want to forget to take with you to the beach.

HELP ME, PLEASE

Check the closet.
On your knees,
under the table,
help me, please,
in that backpack,
search the floor,
in the desk,
behind that door,
on the bookshelf,
on the stairs,
quick, the toilet,
move those chairs,
in the locker,
behind that picture,
check the drawer,
and the light fixture.
Of course I'm sure,
and I'm scared plenty.
I looked there twice.
The cage is empty.

So, when I originally wrote this poem, I was thinking of an empty cage at home and had the reader looking behind the toy box and in the dryer and the fridge. But then I decided to move the poem to school, where it's more important to check out lockers and desks.

Poems are like stories—each has a setting. What if you changed the setting of this poem to a swamp or a baseball stadium? Where would you need to search? The details you choose will set the scene.

Could you write your own poem about searching around for something? Where would YOU look?

CALLED ON

He called on me.
My answer's wrong.
Caught like a squirrel
on an open lawn.

Standing alone,
twiddling my paws,
frozen in place,
working my jaws.

I'd like to bolt,
but where?
I moan.
Could anyone
be more
alone?

Poets take images and turn them into words. A squirrel standing alone, twiddling its paws, is an image. I've seen squirrels do this a gazillion times, but one day it made me think, *That's how I feel when I'm called on.* It's as if I'm all alone, yet the most obvious thing in sight.

Poets always get hung up on the details. I wrote "Good Ears" about my fifth-grade teacher, Mrs. Lockwood. You don't know her, but you know the type. Right?

If I were writing a story about Mrs. Lockwood, I would have also told you that she was nice but smelled like old coffee. But since I was writing a poem, I just zeroed in on the fact that she had excellent ears. Instead of writing about a whole person in your next poem, try writing about just one or two characteristics of that person. Zero in and get real picky about it.

Do you ever feel like some kind of animal? Yes? Which one?

GOOD EARS

My teacher has good ears.
She proves it all the time.
If eight kids fake a sneeze,
she knows which sneeze is mine.

Her back turned toward the class
and writing on the board,
she can even hear the silent drop
of spitballs on the floor.

She doesn't have to turn around
or even look at all
before she says,
"Okay, my friend,
you may stand in the hall."

I think she has to have
a microphone somewhere;
she's picking up on signals
from antennae in her hair.

JUST THINKIN'

Some lessons
you only need once,
like sliding barefoot on a
hardwood floor,
hand placed on a burner,
fingers in a car door.

painful examples

The fact that orange juice and
toothpaste
don't mix
I learned before I could count.
Learned it once.
Learned it quick.
So how come no
amount of instruction
can make
this lesson
stick in my brain?
Smashed fingers
and
splinters might hurt,
but this word list
is really a pain.

THE
RUNNING
START...

YOU DO THE MATH

When the black hole of January stretches and yawns,
don't start counting on your fingers.

$+$ Gray skies, over short days,
plus six more months of school
is an equation that boggles the mind.

─────────────────────────

Infinity defined.

No one owns a sandcastle, and you can't sell a picture drawn in steam, so what's the point?

I once heard a teacher give a speech in which she complained that when she gave students writing assignments they would stare at the wall. She said it as if that were a bad thing.

THE ARTIST, ME

Sandcastles.
Snow writing.
Pictures drawn in steam.
Temporary art
shaped from my daydreams.

Not done for an assignment
or squeezed between the lines.
Imagining is working out,
shaping up the mind.

Staring at the wall is a *good* thing. All good writing comes *after* we bounce ideas around in our brains a little.

She probably knew that, but with the bell schedule and all, she just forgot.

DRIFTING FLAKES

Outside the window,
a field of snow,
the playground, the fence,
that tree
seem as remote as Siberia
to a warm-behind-windows,
mind-skating me.

Don't you forget:
writing isn't just about
working a pencil with
your fingers.

The pine tree catches occasional flurries
in spiky mitts,
molding weighty balls in sagging arms.
That tree has spine!
And, despite the cold,
doesn't moan or whine
as it holds on in the icy swirl
of a windy world
to drifting flakes
(the snow and me),
part moisture and part mystery.

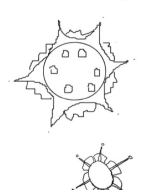

FLAKES
UNITE!

25

ATTRIBUTES

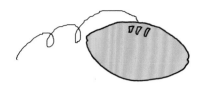

Brown eyes,
fast legs,
and a pair of hoppin' feet.
I like to win
when I take to the court,
but I can take defeat.
I'll play forward or guard,
dribble, pass, shoot.
But to sit on the sidelines?
Does not compute.
One heart, two hands,
I can sink a basketball.
I may not be good at lunch,
but no single attribute
is me.
Instead,
I'm the sum of them all.

What if you were a math problem?
What are your factors?
What are your pluses and minuses?
What is your sum?

Sports. Band. A choir solo. Trying
out has always scared me a little.
I'm afraid of looking like a fool if I
don't make it.

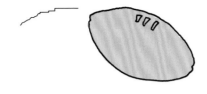

TRYOUTS

If I try out,
what's the worst?
The worst is,
I might lose,
not be the one they choose.

I could say it didn't matter;
I was kidding when I tried.
Then everyone would know
I lost and then I lied.

Or I could shrug and say,
"So what, I lost.
I'm only a beginner."
Besides,
if I never try,
I'll never be a winner.

Poems are places where I lay out
my fears and look them straight in
the eyeballs. The more I stare them
down, the less scary those fears are.

What scares you?
What would you like to try?

I HAVE TO STAND BY SUSAN TODD?

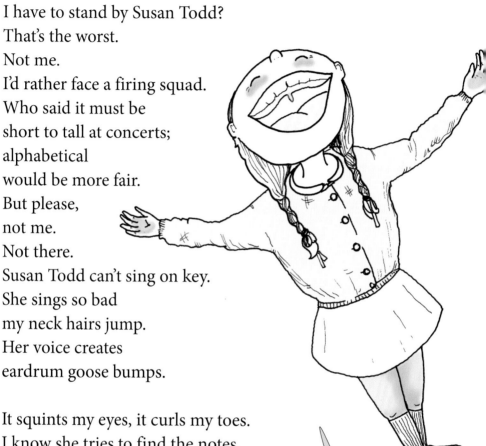

I have to stand by Susan Todd?
That's the worst.
Not me.
I'd rather face a firing squad.
Who said it must be
short to tall at concerts;
alphabetical
would be more fair.
But please,
not me.
Not there.
Susan Todd can't sing on key.
She sings so bad
my neck hairs jump.
Her voice creates
eardrum goose bumps.

It squints my eyes, it curls my toes.
I know she tries to find the notes,
but her screeching search
is like the scrape of blackboards
by a metal rake.

Just this once?
Give me a break.

To write a poem about a feeling,
I have to try that feeling on. To write this
poem, I pretended I was listening to
the worst *American Idol* audition ever.
Sometimes creativity just means taking
time to feel the moment—the good, the
bad, and the screechy.

OH NO!

Sky-blue icing swirls,
a tray of cupcakes,
girls
(two)
passing down the hallway.
It's another student's birthday.
    Cupcakes!
I feel my tummy hop.
Each has a candy top.
Drool puddles on my tongue
while eyeballing which one . . .
    OH NO!
The cupcakes, girls, and tray
    turn left
    and go the other way.
I shatter like a broken glass.

The birthday's in another class.

Can you write a
mouth-watering poem?

Imagery is a picture in words, but it can be
more than that. It can also include smells and
sounds—called *sensory details*. Sensory details
can actually make your nose twitch when you
read them. Or your mouth water.

PACKED AND READY

The teacher says,
    keep it to yourself,
    sit still,
    but she can't hold me down.
'Cause when I
    look inside—
    watch this!—
    I REALLY get around.
There's little space in me
    for assignments,
    clean desks,
    or my locker.
When I'm imagining the weekend,
    a sky of blue,
    a field of green,
    and a kickin' game of soccer.
When the teacher tells us
    please stay seated,
    be quiet, wait for the bell,
    I let out a silent cheer.
Time to pack myself
    in a hands-folded smile,
    and dream
    my way outta here.

I would never write a poem about "sports."

Don't freak out. I just mean if you want to write about sports, you would have to write an encyclopedia, not a poem. Different sports have different terms.

THE GREATEST FUN

Soccer is the greatest fun.
I skinned my shin
and broke my thumb.
I tore my shirt,
my knees are bruised,
my feet both hurt,
my hand's abused,
my clothes are stained,
my head's a pain,
my ankle's sprained,
I'm spitting rain.
Forward or guard
it's just the same,
a low-down, grubby, grimy game
of rarely score
and kick and run.

Soccer is the greatest fun!

But if I'm going to write about one sport and one game, maybe even one moment . . . that's when I would write a poem.

Irony = what you mean is not exactly what you're saying.

Maybe I DO mean that soccer is fun. Or maybe I don't. You decide.

ONE FOR BUBBA

First,
Bubba put his fist in his mouth,
then he belched the alphabet song.
He used his straw for a raisin gun
and hammered his chest,
      just like King Kong.

And then,
Bubba pounded his sandwich into soup
and frog-jumped chair to ledge.
He rolled back both his eyelids
and still couldn't put her
      over the edge.

But when
Bubba blew his pickle breath
in a sandwich bag
and popped it behind her back,
the lunch guard rocketed to the ceiling.
On the way down,
   she finally cracked.

The characters we create for a poem are like characters in a story—they have to be consistent. This means a character like Bubba would not quietly hum the alphabet song (unless he was plotting his next move). That wouldn't be logical.

Bubba's not good at lunch. What's his next move? Watch out!

LEADER OF THE PACK

I dream I am so cool,
a leader of the pack,
friends anywhere I choose
in a finger snap.

In dreams I sparkle
as I win.
I tell jokes
and others grin.

And everybody copies me
and how I dress and talk.
I am followed by my wannabes
every time I walk
from lunch or gym.
I am famous, but still nice.
I am thoughtful and polite.

I know there's pressure
when you're cooler than the rest,
but I can take the stress.
In dreams I'm never warm and flat
like pop left capless in the sun.
That's why dreams are fun.

Sometimes I choose the words of a poem, and sometimes one word chooses another.

Confused? Don't be. For instance, take a look at the first line of this poem, "I dream I am so cool." What does *cool* do? It sparkles (see stanza 2). What would the opposite of *cool* be? Pop left out in the sun (see last stanza).

If you rewrote this poem and began with "I dream I am so hot," what would you substitute when you came to *sparkle*? In the last stanza, what would be the opposite of *hot*? Then think about how it would be to be the hottest kid in school, and finish off the poem.

See how the words *cool* or *hot* help choose the words in the rest of the poem?

Don't like the word *hot*? Try *smooth*, *smart*, *athletic*, or some other description that fits who you are in your dreams.

GETTING GRADED

Opened at school
or opened at home,
report cards
should be private.
No one else should see
or ask,
"Hey, what'd you get?"

I just hold my breath
and peek
and hardly pout or boast.
Just to know is a relief.
I did my best . . .
almost.

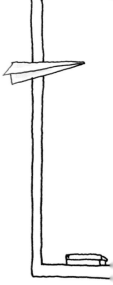

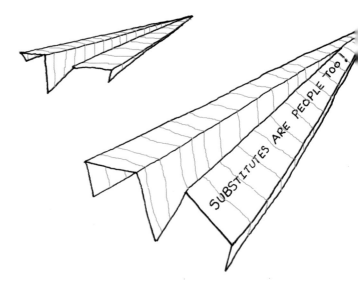

SUBSTITUTES ARE PEOPLE TOO!

Both of these poems have zinger last lines. Kind of like telling a punch line to a joke, you hold back an important piece of information till the very last minute.

The punch line can be funny or offer just a little insight (something the rest of the poem made you think of). You wouldn't want to end every poem with a punch line, but it's fun once in a while.

SUBSTITUTE

Substitute.
Substitute.
Let's trade seats;
pretend you're mute.
Say Jamie's in a coma,
and our teacher
gives no homework.
Say Frankie's deaf
and Cindy's blind.
Hide that chair.
You—over here.
You—over there.
She'll never find
who made her stand.

Rats.
She has a seating plan.

BAD WORDS

Sammy knows bad words.
He uses them to fight.
He knows about a hundred swears
and how to use 'em right.

I don't know where he learned
how to talk that way,
with words that have a sting
but don't have much to say.

BAD WORDS

INTERESTING
GOOD
NICE
WONDERFUL
GREAT
SWEARS

Swear words aren't the only words that don't have much to say. Words that are vague, including a lot of opinion words, are "bad" words. *Great* is a bad word to describe a sunset, because it says nothing about the colors.

So what's the truth about this poem?
Is the speaker *REALLY* a saint?

WHO ME?

I never pass out gossip.
I never peek through doors.
I've never copied homework.
I've never muddied floors.
I never stole a candy,
'specially not before a meal.
I wouldn't spoil my appetite.
Besides,
I never steal.

I never disappoint
or tell a secret
or make another person cry.
I'm practically a saint.
You can trust me.
Would I lie?

Poets tell the truth.
That's what we do.
Most poetry, when you get right down to it, is nonfiction—
a scene, an observation, something we really saw or felt.

Now, sometimes poets take the truth and give it a little twist, which
we call fictionalizing. But at the heart of every poem is a little piece of
truth—a true emotion or an honest response that we communicate to
our readers through an image or a comparison.

The first time I read a poem, I just read the words. The second time I
go looking for the truth. What is the poet really talking about?

100% ME

10% giggles
10% tears
12% confidence
8% fears
2% pizza
3% sighs
30% homework
5% lies
9% messy
6% neat
.6% eyebrows
4.4% feet.

It all adds up, can't you see?
The total is 100% me!

10% + 12% + .6%

Oh, yeah.
You can definitely do this one.
Make a list of what you are (wacky, excited, bored), what
you like (sports, food, clothing, games). Do you like to
laugh? Trampoline? Dunk your brother? Sing out loud?

After you make the list, give each category a percentage.
Hint: do it in pencil, because these are bound to change.
Make sure when you are done that the percentages add
up to 100.

You can make up a totally new first and last line that kind
of sums up who you are.

HOME AND AWAY

Sleep's my friend,
left warm-a-bed
while I'm to school
to fill my head
with haunting bone-pile histories,
algebraic mysteries,
and other take-home tests
I drag back to my nest.

Thoughts wrestle with Sleep,
they pillow fight.
The riot keeps me
up all night.

Dreams can inspire all
kinds of poems. Some
poets even keep a
notebook beside the bed
to write down ideas that
come up in the middle of
the night.

Had a good dream lately?
No?
That's okay.
Nightmares work, too.

MISSING LINKS IN THE FOOD CHAIN

Some creatures
live to give
me spider creeps,
chatter teeth, and
shoulder shakes,
like warty toads
and slippy snakes.
Trashy maggots,
sidewalk worms,
hairy bees, and
bathroom germs.
Slimy slugs
and flappy bats,
sharks with fins
and stick-on gnats.

All fit in nature's
crawly puzzle.
No use asking
why.
But!
Any bug in my hair
or touching my teeth
is probably
going to die.

Poets and scientists often start off in the same place—with a question. Why is this so? How come that's the way that is? Poets and scientists are detectives, trying to solve the mysteries of life.

Poetry! The perfect place to creep someone out.

Poets write about nature all the time. But don't get the idea that all nature poems have to be boring like someone else's vacation pictures from places you've never been. They can be creepy-slippy. Slimy, too. Down and germy. Go for it.

40

ELEMENTS OF DETERMINATION

You may think I'm mostly water,
methane gas,
and two cold feet,
but there's
fifteen tons of pressure
clenched between these teeth.

Be careful of the voltage
if you try and cross my mind.
Part of me's soft tissue,
but
part of me is spine.

For this poem I first made a list of some random science terms. Don't worry. I'm not going to ask you to pick them out of the poem and list them on a worksheet or anything.

Boring!

I'd rather see if you could build a poem from a list of earth science, biology, or geographic terms! You need only about six to get started.

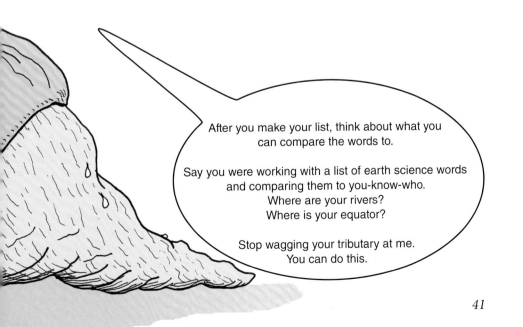

After you make your list, think about what you can compare the words to.

Say you were working with a list of earth science words and comparing them to you-know-who.
Where are your rivers?
Where is your equator?

Stop wagging your tributary at me.
You can do this.

A descriptive poem is like a descriptive paragraph. It just describes something that *is*. It's not really going anywhere; it doesn't have a beginning, middle, or an end—like a narrative story.

PERSPECTIVES

A professional,
well-suited
jay
inspects the ground for his survey.
He clasps both wings
behind his back,
pacing off his earthly map.

Who knew blue jays
gave two squawks
for folded wings
and taking walks?

A poem is like a car, because as soon as someone invented it, others came along and designed new models. This poem is the *quatrain* model. That means it has four lines per stanza. It follows an *a-b-c-b* pattern. The second and fourth lines rhyme.

I may envy him his bird's-eye view,
but (could this be true?)
that flying high
gets boring, too?

Take a look out the window. What do you see? Can you write a descriptive poem about what you see and what you wonder about?

LEAVE-BEHINDS

Q. Who invented poetry?
A. No one knows.

Poetry was invented way before the car or football, even before the invention of writing.

Notice the last line of this poem and how it breaks the pattern. A broken poetry pattern is like a broken sidewalk square: readers kind of trip over it and BAM! You really get their attention.

When you experiment with breaking patterns in your poetry, you draw readers to trip over that particular line, a poet power play that says *Look here!*

Edison thought up the light bulb,
records, and phonographs.
Curie perfected the X-ray;
Knute Rockne, the forward pass.

Salk made vaccinations;
Ford, the Model T;
Disney, Mickey Mouse;
and I—
watch my TV.

I'm nestled in this world
that bold inventors built.
Will my leave-behinds
be just my junk food trash
and guilt?

What made two bicycle makers fly?
What made my couch potato state?
What if I turned off the tube
and let my leisure time create?

I wonder what I'd make.

STORM ALERT

A warning trails across my screen:
>*Warning! Warning! Take cover.*
>*Tornado sighted. Wind and water rising.*

Wish I could evacuate.
Change my name.
Leave the state.
Grumbling.
Thundering.
Storm alert.
>*Homework?*
>*Homework?*

Last night
I managed to
>tune out that voice,
>switched on the tube,
>made the choice

not to read the chapter.
Now it's the morning after.
Storm surge bearing down.
Too late to head for higher ground.
I should have done the work.
Uh-oh.
Teacher twister,
heading for
berserk.

Ever wish you had a crystal ball? A place you could look and predict the future? I think of my writing journal as a kind of crystal ball, because if I write about something I intend to do before I do it, I can better predict what the consequences will be.

Skip homework?
Teacher storm?
Who knew?

IT'S TODAY?

Frantic
panic,
sinking
sorrow.

The science test
is not tomorrow.

The line breaks
in this poem are kind
of misleading because this poem
is really just a couplet (a two-line
rhyming verse). Couplets can be
added together to make a longer
poem, or they can stand alone.

Poet Emily Dickinson
once said, "I hesitate
which word to take,
as I can take but few
and each must be the
chiefest. . . ."

Short poems usually don't start out short—often they begin more like a little story. A happening. Maybe a journal entry. After I have written down the story, then I get busy trimming away the extra words until I find the poem.

Can you imagine a story behind this poem? Your story won't exactly match my original story or the story by the kid sitting next to you, and that's okay. This is called interpretation, and believe me, there is no right or wrong.

When we trim our poems, we are looking to keep the "chiefest" words—the words that tickle our senses or make images in our heads.

MY SHORTEST POEM EVER:

SHAMPOO
BOO HOO

15 FL. OZ

NOT AGAIN!

Redundant.
Redundant.
Quit kicking my desk.
Redundant.
Redundant.
Please stop. You're a pest.
Redundant.
Redundant.
You said that before.
Redundant.
Redundant.
Redundant.
NO MORE!

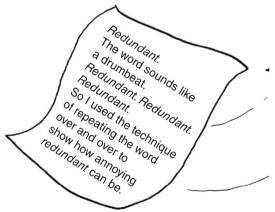

Redundant.
The word sounds like
a drumbeat.
Redundant. Redundant.
Redundant.
So I used the technique
of repeating the word
over and over to
show how annoying
redundant can be.

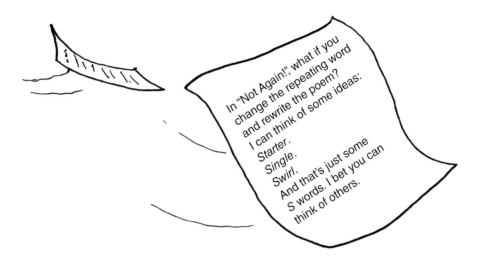

In "Not Again!", what if you change the repeating word and rewrite the poem? I can think of some ideas:
Starter.
Single.
Swirl.
And that's just some S words. I bet you can think of others.

SPELLBOUND

Confluence
and recompense,
aphid,
ibex,
muse,
chrysalis, and zygote.
Words
I know I'll never use.
But, like
gossamer and quell,
I had to learn to spell.

ON BECOMING PROFICIENT

Fact. Fact. Fact.
Hold and cram and stack,
school's a detail-juggling act.
WITH HURDLES!
I'm bound to drop a few.
(Let's face it, you did, too.)

Piled up on my shoulders,
stuck on my shoes
is a swampy collection of
used-to-be news.
It's amazing what schools dredge up
to weigh down my mind and heart,
then invest in a high-stakes test to show
how far behind
I am
before I start.

The sideline's screaming
    PICK UP SPEED
    HURRY UP!
and
    RUN!
But this baton they're passing to me
weighs more than a ton.

When writing, putting
words in all caps is a way
of SCREAMING. Whether
it's timed tests or timed
video games, a ticking
clock makes my brain
freak out and not think
straight, which makes
me want to SCREAM!

It's a personal thing.
But that's the way
poems are.
Personal.

I find sparkles
in the dust
I kick up when I play.
Creative isn't a statistic
or the sum of yesterday.
I came with a personal stopwatch,
let me leave with my self-esteem.
Who needs to race some kid in Iowa?
I'll set my own pace
with plenty of space
to dream.

Psst. No one has ever linked high-proficiency test scores in school to success later in life. Shh. It's a secret.

Here I compare school to a "detail-juggling act. *WITH HURDLES!*"
It is a comparison that does not use the words *like* or *as.* Writers call
that a metaphor.
He's a snake.
She's a Ping-Pong ball.
I'm a coconut.
These metaphors help make an impression, because they force
the reader to make the connection between two different things
through a comparison.

51

WHY ME?

Why me?
     Pick him.
          Or her.
     Or pick me later,
          or not at all.
Better someone else.
Wouldn't you agree?

WHAT?

     Wait a minute.

Wait a minute.

     You picked them?

HEY!

     Why not me?

BE CAREFUL
WHAT YOU WISH FOR.

SWAGGER

Swagger
thinks he's better,
turns his cap toward the back,
curls his lip, refuses to skip
or act like a kid.
Ever.
He's self-assured when he walks in,
full of nerve with a hint of sin,
with one hand in his pocket,
and shoulders square,
and if you don't like it, he doesn't care.
Somewhere between a strut and stroll,
he's on a roll, his step in time
to a silent beat that says "Bring it on,"
'cause he's all that
from his crown to his feet.

Would *Swagger* have
behaved differently if it
had been a girl?

Personification is when writers
put shoes on a thing and
make it walk around, dance,
or jump.

In this poem, I put "shoes"
on the word *swagger* to
see how that word would
behave.

In order to personify
Swagger, I had to imagine
the word as a person
walking into the room all full
of himself.

I'm not sure why I thought of
Swagger as a him and not a her.
For sure, both boys and girls can
swagger. But that's a choice you get
to make when you are the writer.

EVACUATE THE SCHOOL!

Zombies in the bathroom!
There!
I eyeballed them myself.
Shh!
Giant naked desert mole rats
are camped behind that shelf.
Hide!
Lizard Men and Cat People
are prowling down the hall.
The principal's gone werewolf.
Look!
His eyes are red and small.
Ikes!

Math Quiz Today!

What is a horror show but a runaway daydream?

Piranha in the fish tank.
Flying monkeys on the lights.
The librarian's grown fangs.
Duck and cover!
I'm pretty sure she bites.
Freeze!
Aliens are snatching teachers.
The custodian's a ghoul.
This place is freaking out.
Quick!
Evacuate the school.

Summer

CELEBRATE.
JUMP AND SHOUT.
SUMMER'S IN.
SCHOOL IS OUT.